Changes in You and Me

A Book about Puberty, *Mostly for Boys*

Paulette Bourgeois and Kim Martyn

Illustrated by Louise Phillips

KEY PORTER BOOKS

Library and Archives Canada Cataloguing in Publication

Bourgeois, Paulette
 Changes in you and me : a book about puberty, mostly for boys / Paulette Bourgeois.
— Rev. / by Kim Martyn

Includes bibliographic references and index.

ISBN 1-55263-668-2

 1. Puberty—Juvenile literature. 2. Teenage boys—Physiology—
Juvenile literature. 3. Sex instruction for boys—Juvenile literature. I. Martyn, Kim II.
Title.

HQ41.B68 2005   612.6'61

The publisher gratefully acknowledges the support of the Canada Council for the Arts and
the Ontario Arts Council for its publishing program. We acknowledge the support of the
Government of Ontario through the Ontario Media Development Corporation's Ontario
Book Initiative.

We acknowledge the financial support of the Government of Canada through the Book
Publishing Industry Development Program (BPIDP) for our publishing activities.

Key Porter Books Limited
Six Adelaide Street East, Tenth Floor
Toronto, Ontario
Canada M5C 1H6

www.keyporter.com

Text design: Peter Maher
Electronic formatting: Jean Lightfoot Peters

Printed and bound in Canada

05 06 07 08 09 6 5 4 3 2 1

Acknowledgments

The authors would like to acknowledge all the wonderful adolescents, parents, teachers and health professionals who so thoughtfully answered many difficult and challenging questions. Friends and their children were forthcoming with anecdotes, questions and suggestions. We are grateful to Key Porter for their full support of a book about puberty that "tells it all" candidly and with humor. Linda Pruessen's vision for the revised edition was right on.

We are grateful to Dr. Martin Wolfish and Dr. David Lloyd, consultants in pediatrics and adolescent medicine, who reviewed the original manuscript and made valuable comments. We also thank Father Bob Moran, Mary Scandrett, Erica Glossop, Elizabeth Anne Gordon, Jane Somerville, Patrick Crean, Jennifer Glossop, Bettina Federspiel, Lyba Spring, Lillian Stermac and Mark.

Note to the Reader

Welcome to your life! We've written this book for youth who want to know a bit more about this time called *puberty*. In this book we try to give you some information about the physical, emotional and social changes that people go through during puberty. As you can see from the title, this book focuses mainly on boys. (There is a section about what happens to girls as well, in case you're curious.) Everybody will go through puberty in their own way, at their own speed, so you may already know some of the information in this book, and some you may not be interested in until later. When talking about bodies and sexual matters people use lots of different kinds of words—slang, dictionary, polite and baby talk. In this book we use mostly dictionary or medical words so that you'll know the "real" terms. Since you've been taught the dictionary words for other parts of your body, like "elbow," you may as well know the words for the reproductive and sexual parts, too!

There may be words you don't understand or cannot pronounce. Look in the glossary at the end of the book for an explanation of the words that appear in *italics*.

If some of the language or content in this book grosses you out or offends you, we apologize. However, we think that with a topic as important as this, it's a good idea to be as clear as possible.

Note to Parents, Caregivers and Other Caring Adults

While this book was written for boys ages 9 to 13, you may also find some of it interesting! We apologize in advance for any offense taken regarding the language or content used in the text. We think that it is important that young people clearly understand this information, and at times that means including terms that are commonly used. We have also included topics that may be beyond your child's years at this point but may not be a couple of years from now. Please see For More Information on page 57.

Contents

1 A Time of Change

Every girl and boy goes through a stage of life called *adolescence*. This weird and wonderful time exists between childhood and adulthood. As you pass through it, you experience changes: you become more independent; you start to sort out your feelings about yourself, your friends and your family. You make decisions about how you want to look, things like smoking or drinking and what to do when you like someone. You also experience the physical changes of growing up. This book is about all these changes. It is about puberty.

You probably already know a lot about your body, and about girls' bodies and even about the changes of puberty. Here's a quiz for you to test yourself.

True or False?

1. Puberty is the same as sexuality.	T	F
2. It takes years for all the changes to happen.	T	F
3. A growth spurt is the first sign of puberty.	T	F
4. Boys sometimes have periods.	T	F
5. Guys who start puberty early end up with bigger penises.	T	F
6. Boys sometimes talk with their dads about these changes.	T	F
7. If you eat vitamins, you can speed up puberty.	T	F
8. Most boys start puberty before age 11.	T	F
9. Both guys and girls get mood swings during this stage of life.	T	F
10. The area under a boy's nipples may become temporarily puffy or sensitive.	T	F

ANSWERS: 1.F, 2.T, 3.F, 4.F, 5.F, 6.T, 7.F, 8.F, 9.T, 10.T

Puberty and Sexuality

Puberty is different from *sexuality*. Puberty means the changes that happen inside and outside our bodies as we mature so that, if we want to, we can reproduce when we're older.

Sexuality is a huge part of who you are, from the moment you're born until the end of your life. It has to do with *gender*, being *male* or *female*. Of course it includes the reproductive parts of our body, which are needed to make babies. For males this means the *testicles* and a *penis*. Sexuality also has to do with how comfortable you are with yourself and your body. Another part has to do with whom we become sexually attracted to, called *orientation*. And the part that makes many young people laugh is the sexual feelings we get and may, later on, share with another person. Some people refer to this *aroused* feeling as being *horny*.

People have *sexual intercourse* for pleasure and to make babies. Some common words for sexual intercourse are making love, *sex*, having sex, doing it, sleeping together and going all the way. There are many more slang terms you've likely heard! Before two people have sexual intercourse, they usually kiss and touch each other above and below the waist. This is sometimes called *making out* or *fooling around*.

As we mentioned, sexuality isn't just about sex. As a baby you needed to be touched and held just to survive. As you grew, you learned the kind of touches that made you feel warm and loved and the kind of touches you didn't like. Hugs can feel great. But a hug when you don't want one feels uncomfortable. Sometimes even nice touches turn into uncomfortable touches. Have you ever been tickled and yelled, "Stop!" but the person kept tickling you? Not fun.

When Does Puberty Start?

Puberty takes a long time from beginning to end, about three to five years. There is no "right age" and there's no way to speed it up or slow it down.

Puberty starts for most boys sometime between the ages of 9 and 14. No two people go through puberty in exactly the same way. In every sixth grade classroom, there are boys who are nearing the end of puberty and boys who are just beginning. That's usual.

If you start puberty much before the age of 9 or show no signs of it by the time you are 14, your parents can mention it to your doctor.

What Changes Happen in Puberty?

Stage 1.

Your *scrotum* (sack) gets darker, gets less smooth-looking and hangs lower. Inside, the testicles get bigger.

Stage 2.

You want to sleep in longer and eat more. You may wonder why your moods go wacky. Fine, straight *pubic hair* grows around the base of your penis. Underarm hair starts to grow. You sweat more and the sweat smells stronger. Temporary *nipple* changes (puffy, sore) happen in 60 percent of guys.

Stage 3.

Your *genitals* continue to grow, with one testicle hanging lower than the other. Upper lip "fuzz" starts. Your voice begins to "crack"—gets high-pitched and then low. The growth spurt you've been waiting for kicks in and you may also have new attractions to other people. Pimples and oilier hair are common.

Stage 4.

Your shoulders and neck widen, and you become more muscular. Pimples may appear on your back and shoulders. Your penis gets wider, and your testicles start to make *sperm*. You have more *erections*, and you *ejaculate semen*. Your face looks more adult.

What Will I Look Like?

Something I like about the way I look now is............... (name at least one thing, even if you don't want to write it down)

What determines how you will look when you grow up? How tall you become, your hair color, the size of your penis, skin type and your overall shape depend mostly on your *heredity*. This means the *genes* you got from your birth parents. For example, if all of your blood relatives are tall, it is likely you will be, too. If all of your relatives are short, there's a good chance that's how you'll be when you're an adult.

Aside from genetics, our looks also depend on what food we eat and how active we are. There's more on this in Chapter 5.

During puberty, parts of your body grow at different times, so be patient if your nose or toes seem to have sprung ahead of the rest of you!

As you know, some people go to a lot of effort to change the way they naturally look. Unfortunately we hear lots of put-downs about people's bodies—their weight, height, hair, skin and clothes. These comments put us all under a lot of pressure to look just a certain way. If you watch TV and look at magazines you'll notice the actors and models almost all have a certain "look." The guys are mainly young and "well built," with full heads of hair. Many of the females are slim and have perky *breasts*. Everyone knows this isn't how real people look. We come in all ages, shapes and sizes. The challenge is to like what you have and not pay too much attention to the pressure you may feel to change yourself. Sure it's fun to look different in some way, just be careful not to lose yourself!

How Will I Feel?

Most boys ask, "Am I normal? Does anyone else feel this way?" The answer is almost always yes, even though you think you are acting, feeling or growing in a way that seems different from other people your age.

When you begin to notice that you're changing you may feel like letting others know, or you may not. When the changes begin to be noticeable some boys feel kind of proud or happy, others feel shy or even wish the changes weren't happening. How you feel depends on lots of things, particularly on

other people's reactions. If you are constantly teased or bullied because you are changing somewhat faster or slower than others, it's hard to feel excited. Sometimes even family members make such a big deal about puberty that it can be embarrassing.

However, if the people around you react appropriately, it's much easier to feel fine about the changes.

You might think you are the only person feeling weird about puberty. You're not alone! If there is one common thing about puberty, it is that almost everybody worries about being normal. Boys and girls all spend a lot of time comparing themselves to others. Remember that everybody goes through puberty in their own way, at their own speed.

The chances are good that everything you are experiencing is perfectly normal. And, hopefully, you don't have to worry about being teased or bullied. But if you are worried, or are being bothered by others, talk with someone in your family, a doctor, a teacher, a youth leader or a counselor. There are also hotline numbers on page 57 that may be of help. Guys often mention something to a friend. This is fine, it's just that people your age may not have all the information they need. And while it's also true that adults sure don't know everything, they'll usually do their best to help.

Talk It Over

Talking with your dad or mom (yes, your mom!) may be helpful. It also makes it more likely that they will trust you as you get older and want more freedom. Here are a couple of questions you can ask them if they are shy:

1. "When you were growing up, how did you find out about all this puberty stuff?"
2. "As a teen what kind of skin did you have—clear, or lots of pimples?"

2 Your Changing Body

Most of you know about the obvious signs of puberty, but what's happening inside your body is not as easy to understand.

Raging Hormones

Some Important Glands

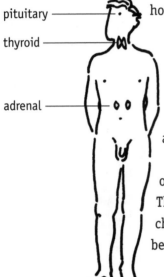

pituitary

thyroid

adrenal

Hormones are powerful chemical messengers in your body. They are made in special *glands* and travel through the bloodstream. Each hormone has a specific job. When you are about to run a race, before you start, you feel your heart pounding and your body suddenly bursting with energy. This happens because a certain hormone is released. There are different hormones that make puberty happen.

Deep inside your brain there is an organ smaller than a gum ball called the *pituitary gland*. It acts as a master switch and "turns on" your body to make sex hormones for the first time.

Boys and girls both make the same sex hormones—*estrogen, progesterone* and *testosterone*. Boys make lots of testosterone and a small amount of progesterone and estrogen, while it is the opposite for girls.

You can thank hormones for making your oil and *sweat glands* work overtime, giving you stronger body odor and more oily skin and hair. They can change the way you feel, too. You might have sudden mood changes. You might have more sexual thoughts about other people because of your hormones.

It's testosterone that tells your testicles to wake up and start producing sperm—which is a pretty big part of growing up male.

Your Sex Organs

The sex organs have many names, including genitals and *reproductive organs*. Some of the reproductive organs hang outside your body and others are on the inside.

You have two testicles, or *testes*. Common slang terms are *balls* or *nuts*. They are firm, oval-shaped organs. Before puberty they are each the size of a boy's thumb, and they grow to be the size of a plum.

Your scrotum is a bag of skin that hangs outside your body and holds your testicles. Often this is just called your "bag" or "sack."

The *urethra* is a long narrow tube that carries *urine* from the *bladder* through the penis and out of the body. Semen also travels from the testes through this tube.

Your *epididymis* consists of long tubes that are tightly coiled around the back of each *testis*. Sperm mature in these tubes.

The head of your penis is called the *glans*. In boys who have not been *circumcised*, it is covered with a fold of skin called the *foreskin*. Inside your penis there is spongy tissue and passageways for extra blood.

Your *prostate gland* and *seminal vesicles* make fluid that mixes with the sperm to make semen. This gives sperm the energy and protection they need to survive once they leave your body.

Sperm ducts (also called the *vas deferens*) are long narrow tubes between your epididymis and your urinary opening.

The *ampulla* is a kind of a holding tank, where sperm are stored until they are ejaculated.

Your *bladder* is the organ that stores your urine (pee).

The *anus* is the opening through which *bowel movements* (poop) pass from your intestines.

Male Sex Organs

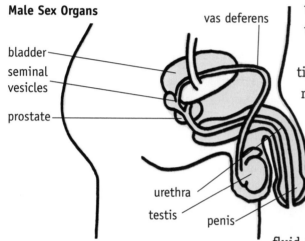

vas deferens

bladder

seminal vesicles

prostate

urethra

testis

penis

3 More about Your Genitals

Most guys spend a lot of time thinking about their penis. Some give it a name, some play with it and some worry if their penis is "normal."

Here are penis facts you should know. Most penises are an average size and shape. In a fully grown male, the average penis, when erect, is about 5.5 to 6 inches (14 to 15 cm) long. When it's soft, it's much smaller. And there are lots of variations in penis skin tone, how it curves, the angle it has when erect and how the end, or head, looks. If you have a penis that looks quite different from any others you've seen, remember there is no "normal" when it comes to bodies. The size and shape of a penis has nothing to do with being "manly," peeing, being a good lover or becoming a father. Girls and other guys make lots of jokes about penises, especially size, but as the saying goes, "It's not the wand, it's the wizard that matters."

Can You Spot the Myths?

1. There's a bone inside your penis. That's why it gets hard.
2. If you masturbate too much, you'll use up all your sperm.
3. You can tell the size of a guy's penis just by looking at the size of his hands and feet, or his nose.
4. All guys have wet dreams.
5. Females only like guys who have big penises.
6. It's better to be circumcised.
7. The bigger your testicles, the more sperm you make.

ANSWERS: Not one of the above statements is true.

16

Circumcised   **Uncircumcised**   **Foreskin Pulled Back**

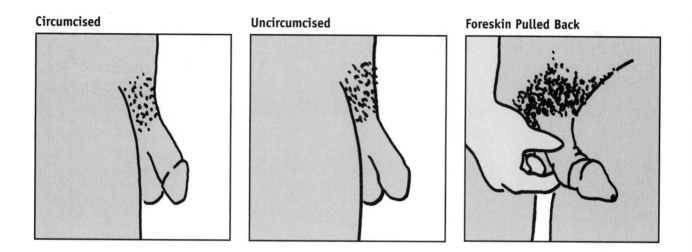

Circumcision

Circumcision is an operation that cuts away the foreskin at the end of the penis. In Jewish, Muslim and some other faiths and cultures, it is a custom to circumcise baby boys. In some cultures, it is a test of manhood to remove a youth's foreskin during a traditional initiation ceremony. In some families it is done because that is the family's custom.

Unless it is for religious or cultural reasons, most medical professionals today do not recommend circumcision.

Whether you are circumcised or not does not change the way your penis works. However, if you are not circumcised, you must gently roll back the foreskin and wash away the white substance called *smegma*. It is a lubricant that is produced by the body so the foreskin can move. If smegma is not washed away, it can become smelly or cause an infection. Also, once a male starts to have sex, if he has a foreskin he needs to be aware that he is at higher risk of *sexually transmitted infections* if he does not use condoms consistently.

Jockstraps and getting hit in the _____!

As all guys know, getting hit in the crotch is a *terrible* feeling! In the case of a really serious hit, that feeling goes away but permanent damage can be done inside the testicles. This kind of contact often happens during certain sports, so guys are given jockstraps to wear. A jockstrap, and the protective cup that fits inside, holds your scrotum close to your body so your testicles are less likely to be hit or bruised during exercise or sports.

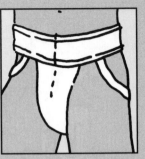

The Inside Story

As you know, your scrotum is the wrinkled bag of skin that hangs outside the body and holds the testicles. One testis usually hangs lower than the other (so they don't bang against each other when you walk), and one may be bigger than the other. Each testis is filled with tightly coiled thin tubes called tubules. If you could straighten out all the tubules in your testicles, they would stretch the length of two football fields!

During puberty, your brain sends out a signal to the testicles to tell them to wake up and start making sperm. They will continue to do so for the rest of your life. After puberty, guys make about 400 million sperm a day. Each sperm is so small you can see it only under a microscope. Five hundred sperm lying head to tail are only about 1 inch (2.5 cm) long!

You may wonder why such important organs—testes—are left on the outside of the body with no protection. All of our other key organs are well protected by bone and muscle. There is a reason. Sperm can only be made at a temperature slightly below body temperature. So, hanging in the scrotum on the outside of the body is cooler. And that's why your scrotum pulls up closer to your body after a cold swim, so the sperm won't get too cold.

Every day the fresh sperm start a five- to six-week journey through the long, coiled epididymis behind each testis. Sperm need this time to become mature. Once the sperm are mature, they travel up the vas deferens and have other fluid added to help them live. They end up in the ampulla, where they stay until they are either ejaculated or die off.

Because sperm are in the body for quite a while as they are maturing, scientists have discovered that certain exposure to radiation and some

About Sperm

A sperm is a male sex cell. It has one job: to join with a female sex cell, which is called an egg or ovum.

A sperm has a head that contains its genetic material and a tail that helps it swim. Unlike some pictures you may have seen, they don't have eyes and brains! Sperm can't survive or move unless they mix with other fluid made in the prostate and seminal vesicles. This fluid is like Gatorade for sperm. It is full of sugar and nutrients that keep sperm healthy and active.

chemicals, such as those found in cigarettes, can harm the sperm. So if a guy wants to help make a healthy baby some day, he needs to be aware of his health, too, not just the mother's.

If a male has only one testis (sometimes a boy is born this way and sometimes accidents or, rarely, cancer cause the loss), then the remaining testis can still make enough sperm for him to get a woman *pregnant*.

Erections

From the time you were an infant (even before you were born!) you had erections. They happen when you wake up in the morning and when your bladder is full and you have to pee. They also happen when you feel excited and even sometimes when you are anxious or frightened.

How does an erection, commonly called a *boner* or hard-on, happen? Well, when your penis is soft, there's blood flowing inside it just like all body parts. In order to become hard, extra blood flows in and then the muscles at its base tighten and trap blood inside. Your penis stands out

Flaccid

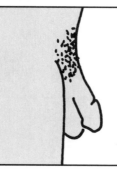

Partially erect

Erect

from your body and gets darker, larger and harder. The erection may last for seconds, minutes or longer, like half an hour. You might be afraid your penis will break, because it is so hard. It won't. Then, after a while your muscles relax and your penis softens.

During puberty, you'll find you have "spontaneous" erections. Some guys get embarrassed when they have an erection around other people, but it's not noticeable (unless you're wearing a bathing suit or sweats with no underwear)! To make it go down, ignore it or think about something boring, like helping with chores.

Ejaculation and Orgasm

"What's a wet dream?" — GRADE 7 CLASS

"Is it only guys who come?" —YOUTH GROUP, AGED 10–14

One thing that happens only to guys, and never to girls, is the production of sperm.

So how do you know when you've started to make sperm? At some point your penis becomes erect and spurts out a small amount of whitish sticky fluid—semen. This is called *ejaculation*, commonly referred to as coming or cuming, because the semen comes out. The semen is also often called *cum*.

Ejaculation can happen at different times. Many boys experience it first during a *wet dream*, which is really called a nocturnal emission. "Nocturnal" means nighttime and "emission" means to send forth or release. You might be dreaming about something sexual, or frightening or exciting like a race. Your heart beats faster, there is an increase in the blood flow to the genitals and you get an erection. At some point there is a series of quick muscle contractions from the testicles to the penis and your semen is released. When you wake up, surprise, there is a small wet spot on your sheets or night wear. At first you may think, "Great, I've wet my bed," but then you see that the wet spot is whitish, not yellow, and

Ejaculation occurs when sperm mixes with seminal fluid and leaves the body through the urethra.

Ejaculation

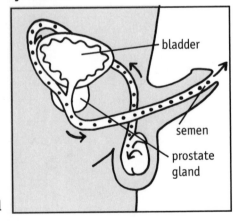

- bladder
- semen
- prostate gland

20

it doesn't smell like urine. Once you realize it's semen you can relax, because it's just a normal part of growing up. Put the wet stuff in the laundry bin (you may want to mention something to your parents so they'll know not to ask too many questions). Not all guys have wet dreams, but most do.

Another time when ejaculation may happen is when you masturbate or rub you penis because it feels good. There's more about this in the next chapter. Also in that chapter is a discussion about sexual activity.

In order for a baby to be made, a man must ejaculate into a woman's vagina.

Some guys may worry that they will "cum" whenever they get an erection. This will not happen. If you are around someone who you think is hot and you get an erection, you won't end up with a wet spot on your pants!

Along with the release of semen, most males will experience an *orgasm* at the time of ejaculation. This is an intense, pleasurable feeling that runs through the whole body. While they usually happen at the same time, ejaculation and orgasm aren't the same thing. For instance, before he produces semen a boy may still self-pleasure and have an orgasm (even little boys). To answer the question at the beginning of this section (on page 20), only males make and ejaculate semen, but females can have orgasms.

4 Sex and Pregnancy

From the moment we are born we are all sexual beings. Once puberty happens, not only do you have the potential to reproduce, but you may find you think more about romance and sexual stuff. You may wonder what it's like to be in love and kiss somebody. Sexual thoughts, fantasies, curiosity and *masturbation* (or self-exploration) are common for guys and girls as they grow up.

Masturbation/Self-Exploration

Throughout our lives we try to figure out how our bodies work and what feels nice.

Some guys rub and touch their genitals. This is called masturbation. You'll hear lots of jokes about this, especially from other guys who give it lots of names, including *jerking off* or "playing with yourself." People (males and females) self-pleasure for lots of reasons: in order to explore how their body works, for pleasure, to release a buildup of sexual feelings and to relax. An orgasm, which often happens when a man rubs his penis, helps create a relaxed feeling.

Unlike some stories you may have heard, self-exploration won't cause any physical harm. In fact, regular self-pleasuring has been found to reduce the risk of prostate cancer in older men. Some adults and religious teachings say that this kind of self-pleasuring is not okay. Part of growing up involves deciding what you believe and what you feel comfortable doing, or not doing. It's your body, so it's up to you to figure it out.

When Can You Have Sex?

It is possible for people to have sexual intercourse and make babies as soon as boys make sperm and girls start to *ovulate*. But does this mean it's a good time to start? You're likely saying "No way!" and you're right. For guys and girls, sex should wait until they mature. Sexuality is a gift, and you need to understand it before sharing it. There's more about the serious side of sex in Chapter 9.

Orientation

Transsexual refers to a person who looks like one gender on the outside but feels like the other gender . . . complicated!

Who you are emotionally and sexually attracted to is referred to as your orientation. This is different than your *gender*, which refers to being male or female. People who are mainly attracted to members of the opposite sex are called *heterosexual* or *straight*. Those who are mainly attracted to the same sex are called *homosexuals*, with *lesbian* as the female term and *gay* as the male term. And just to make it very complex, there are people who are interested in both men and women. The term for this is *bisexual*.

a good question

"Why are some people gay?" —GRADE 8 STUDENT

Nobody really knows the answer to this question. The same goes for the question, "Why are most people straight?" What we do know is that we do not choose our orientation; it's something that just is the way it is.

When we grow up it is common to have a strong attraction to other males, such as a friend, teacher or actor. As you get older, these feelings may continue or not. If you are ever confused about the thoughts and feelings you have as you get older please talk to an adult you trust, or call a talk line for youth. Often what you're experiencing is perfectly normal, just new to you!

a good question

How can two women have sex?" —GRADE 6 CLASS

People of all orientations may fall in love and share their lives together. When people decide to share themselves in a sexual way they may hug, touch, kiss and have sex with each other. They use all different parts of their body to do this. The big difference is that if there isn't a penis and a vagina, then that kind of intercourse doesn't happen. And without sperm and an egg the couple could not make their own child.

Having Sex—Making Love

Sexual intercourse between a woman and a man is usually the way people make babies. It is also a way they can give and get physical pleasure.

When two people are ready and want to be as close as possible to each other, they may have sexual intercourse. They touch, stroke and kiss each other until the man's penis becomes larger and erect and the woman's *vagina* becomes wet and slippery from special fluids her body makes.

The man slides his penis inside the woman's vagina and moves his penis in and out until semen, called cum, spurts out. This is called ejaculation. The kissing, rubbing and touching usually give the man an orgasm. The woman may also have an orgasm. Once the man has ejaculated, his penis will again become smaller and soft and slip out of the *vagina*.

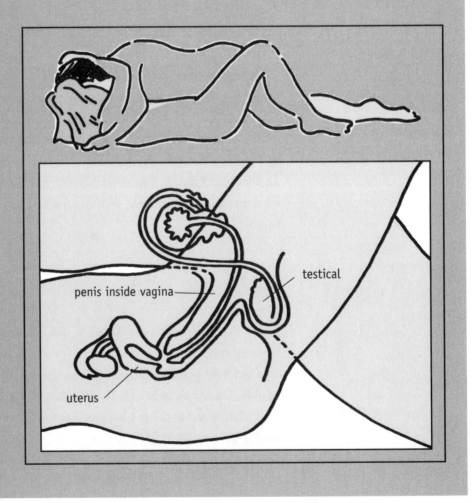

testical

penis inside vagina

uterus

Fertilization: How Pregnancy Starts

The ovum is the largest human cell—the only one you can see with your eyes. This is about the size of an ovum. →•

You've likely heard about females making *ova* or "eggs," which are needed to make a baby. And you already know that guys make sperm cells. These cells carry the codes for creating human life. These are called genes. The genes contain messages for cells about how they should grow and act. The ovum has the genes from the mother. A sperm cell carries genes from the father.

During sexual intercourse between a man and a woman, when the semen is ejaculated, about 400 million sperm race to fertilize the ovum (egg). The journey takes hours, and most sperm die off before they reach the *fallopian tubes*. And if there is no ovum in the tube at that time, then there is no pregnancy.

As soon as one sperm enters the egg, no other sperm can enter. The sperm and the egg join together. The egg is fertilized. This is also called *conception*. The fertilized egg then travels down the tube and attaches to the inside of the *uterus*. From now until it is nine weeks old, it is called an *embryo*.

a good question

"Is there any other way of getting pregnant than having you-know-what"?
—GRADE 5 STUDENT

When you're younger you can't imagine having sex, even if you want to have kids. Those feelings generally disappear once you get older. However, some people can't get pregnant through sexual intercourse, and so they may get some extra help. Artificial insemination is when sperm is put into a woman's vagina. In vitro fertilization occurs when the egg is removed by a doctor and fertilized by a sperm outside of the woman's body. It is then put in the uterus to grow.

How Does a Woman Know She's Pregnant?

Since the embryo is attached inside the uterus, a woman stops getting her *period* when she is pregnant. She may feel tired, have tender breasts, pee more often and feel nauseated (want to throw up). However, lots of women don't feel much different for quite a while.

The only sure way for somebody to know they are pregnant is to do a urine test. These are available at a doctor's office or clinic, or for sale at drugstores.

Being Pregnant

You often hear people say that the baby is growing in the mother's stomach, but of course that's not true! It's growing in a special place—the uterus.

The embryo grows quickly inside a sac filled with *amniotic fluid*. Here it floats, kicks and sleeps. It gets oxygen and nutrients and gets rid of its body waste through the *placenta*, an organ it shares with the mother. The embryo is attached to the placenta by the *umbilical cord*. Because the embryo totally depends on what comes from the mother, it's *very important* that she eat well and avoid chemicals and drugs, such as alcohol.

After nine weeks of growing, the embryo is called a *fetus*. It is the size of a peanut, and it has a bulgy head, internal organs, tiny arms and legs, fingers and a face.

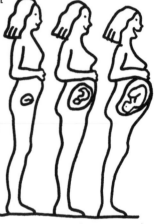

12 weeks   24 weeks   40 weeks

Giving Birth

About nine months after *fertilization*, the baby is ready to be born. The mother's uterus is a powerful muscle. It tightens and relaxes until the baby is pushed out of the uterus. The opening in the *cervix* expands until it is wide enough for the baby's head. This is called labor—which is a good word to use since it means "work"! It is exciting and tiring. Women are encouraged to focus on deep breathing and relaxing during labor. There are also certain positions, massage techniques and medicines to help with the birth process.

Do you know the story of your birth?

Usually, the baby's head comes out first, and then the rest of the body slides out. The blood supply from the umbilical cord shuts off, and blood races to the lungs so the baby can breathe. The umbilical cord, which has no feeling, is cut. The placenta and cord are also pushed out of the mother's body because they are no longer needed. After a few days, the remaining bit of the cut umbilical cord still attached to the baby's belly falls off. The scar that is left is called a belly button, or navel.

Some babies are born by *cesarean section* because they cannot be born through the vagina. The mother is given an anesthetic to numb her lower body, an incision (cut) is made through her uterus, the baby is lifted out and the mom gets stitches.

About Twins

There are two kinds of twins: fraternal and identical. Fraternal twins do not necessarily look alike while identical twins are, well, identical! Sometimes, two eggs are released into the fallopian tubes at ovulation. They are each fertilized by a different sperm. Two separate embryos, each with its own placenta, start to develop. These are fraternal twins.

Identical twins develop when one egg divides into two identical halves soon after fertilization. They share a placenta, but each has their own sack. The babies are born one at a time, often through a vaginal birth.

Conjoined or Siamese babies are identical twins that did not fully separate.

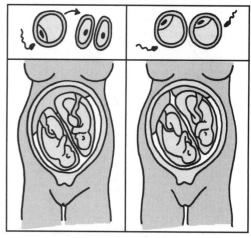

Identical Twins   **Fraternal Twins**

About Miscarriage

Sometimes a woman is pregnant and things are not going as they should inside. Her body will end the pregnancy with a *miscarriage* or spontaneous abortion. It will be as though she's having a very heavy period. This usually happens within the first three months, but it may be so early that she hasn't even discovered that she is pregnant yet. One in four pregnancies ends this way. If she wants to, the woman can go ahead and get pregnant again in a short while.

A *stillbirth* happens when the fetus dies when it is mostly made but not born yet. The delivery happens, but the baby is not alive. Fortunately, this does not happen very often.

How Breasts Make Milk

Inside a woman's breasts are tiny pockets called alveoli where milk is made by special milk-making cells. After a woman gives birth to a baby, hormones tell her alveoli to make milk. When a mother holds her baby next to her breast, the baby starts to suck on her nipple. The sucking draws the milk from the alveoli, through the milk ducts and out small holes in the nipple. The mother will keep making milk as long as she breast-feeds (nurses) her baby. When a mother stops breast-feeding her baby, her breasts stop making milk.

5 Growing Up

From the moment you started life, you were growing. At puberty, hormones start to control your body shape. For guys, testosterone is the key player. As you know, there are other factors that influence how your body will grow. How much and what kinds of food you eat, how physically active you are and how much sleep you get all affect your development.

About Bones

The long bones of your body—arm bones, leg bones, finger and toe bones—have rubbery cartilage at each end. It grows and makes your bones longer. At puberty, testosterone makes the cartilage grow quickly and then stop. This period of quick growth is called a growth spurt.

By the time puberty is over, there is a small cushion of cartilage at the ends of your bones. The rest of the bone is hard. When that happens, you stop growing taller.

Getting Taller

Weird!

As you know from looking around, men come in all different heights. When you are growing at your fastest, you will grow about 2 to 4 inches (5 to 10 cm) in one year. No wonder your pants start to look too short! Guys usually start their growth spurt when they are about 11 or 12 years old, while most girls start earlier. Guys continue to grow until they are about age 18, and girls finish growing by age 16.

If you start getting taller early, it does not mean you'll be a giant when you're older. You will grow only as tall as you are meant to grow, depending on the genes you have inherited.

Your body won't grow at the same rate all over. Your feet might suddenly grow two sizes. You can start to borrow your dad's shoes! Then your hands will get bigger. Your face gets longer. Your chin and nose stick out more. Your shoulders widen. Your other bones lengthen and you develop more muscles. You might feel like some weird cartoon character who keeps being redrawn!

Voice Changes

Your voice box, the *larynx*, grows during puberty. You will notice your Adam's apple sticking out more in the middle of your neck. As your larynx and the muscles inside become thicker and longer, your voice deepens. Sometimes, a boy's voice changes smoothly and gradually, but many boys find that their voices "crack" during this time. One moment they have a deep voice, and the next they have a high, squeaky voice. Your voice will even out as your larynx matures.

larynx

About Breasts

Although girls have the most noticeable breast development during puberty, boys' breasts change as well. Your *areola*, the area around your nipple, becomes wider and darker, and your nipple gets larger. You may notice that your chest is tender and there may be small bumps and swelling.

More than half the boys going through puberty notice some swelling. You are not growing breasts: this is a common part of puberty and can last for a year or two. If the swelling does not disappear after that time, talk to you doctor.

Eating for Health and Fun

Going through all of this changing uses up a lot of energy. This is why when you go through puberty, you will notice an increase in your appetite. You start to open the fridge door to see what's there more often! If you are starting your growth spurt, you'll need that extra food energy for strong bones and muscles.

You've heard about healthy eating, but what does it mean? No fries or hamburgers? No sweets? No. It means eating a variety of foods and cutting down on sugar, fried foods, fatty foods and salt.

Unlike many adults, you probably don't go around thinking, "Oh, this is full of fiber so I'll have lots of it!" But it is good to have some idea of what healthy eating looks like. You probably know that it's a good idea to eat a variety of foods—milk products such as milk, yogurt and ice cream; fresh fruits and vegetables; pasta, rice, bread and cereal; and meat protein or alternatives such as tofu, beans, peanuts and nuts. If you have a choice, pick intense-colored vegetables such as spinach, broccoli, carrots and squash, and orange fruits such as cantaloupe and oranges. And instead of just grabbing high-fat snacks like chocolate bars and potato chips, pick a handful of nuts, a bowl of popcorn (maybe with a sprinkling of cheese), carrot sticks or some yogurt.

If you're always feeling hungry, resist reaching for a quick fix like cookies or a pop. Try to eat more protein as well as more rice, noodles, potatoes, pasta or whole-grain breads at your meals.

Breakfast

Can you pick the best breakfast for a teenage guy?

1. One fried egg, two strips of bacon, a glass of orange juice, a glass of milk and one slice of whole-wheat bread with butter and jam.
2. Two slices of leftover pizza (with extra cheese, mushrooms and green peppers) with a glass of juice (not fruit "drink").
3. A bowl of cereal with raisins and rice milk, a slice of cantaloupe and a glass of orange juice with calcium.
4. Hot chocolate with milk (not water), and a bagel with peanut butter and banana.

ANSWER: All the breakfasts have a variety of foods you need—breads or cereals, fruits or veggies, and some meat or alternatives. Breakfast 1 is not a good choice for every day because the butter and bacon add extra fat you don't need.

The Question of Calcium

Which one of the following gives you the amount of calcium needed each day for a guy going through puberty?

1. Four glasses of milk.
2. Four glasses of fortified soy drink.
3. A large piece of cheddar cheese and a milkshake made with two glasses of milk and one scoop of ice cream.

ANSWER: All of them! Remember, because your bones are growing, you need more calcium than children and adults.

What about Sleep?

Did you know that our bones grow the most during our sleeping hours?

Do you yawn through most of your classes and fall asleep late at night watching TV? Chances are you are not getting enough sleep. Your body needs to be both active and get enough sleep to feel healthy and alert. While it's true that different people need different amounts of sleep, some doctors recommend that adolescents get 10 hours of sleep each night.

It's hard as you get older because you'll find that you want to stay up later and later, but you still need to get up for school! You have to find a balance. If you're tired all the time it could be your diet, activity level, emotional state—or lack of time in the sack! If your parents have a set bedtime for you, but you toss and turn because you're not tired and you wake up before the alarm goes off, perhaps you can talk about a later bedtime.

About Exercise

Every day you need at least 90 minutes of physical activity—how much do you get now?

It doesn't matter what kind of exercise you choose—a team sport, biking, walking, dancing, swimming, skating—as long as you do something. Your bones and muscles need exercise to grow properly. Lots of kids find that exercise helps them think more clearly and better handle all the stresses of school, friendships and family. Guys who participate in a physical activity find they don't get bored as often as kids who hang around with "nothing to do."

About Muscles and Strength

When you were born, one-fifth of your body was muscle. At the beginning of puberty, your body was one-quarter muscle. It will be almost half muscle by the time you're an adult.

Muscles allow your body to move. They are made of long, thin cylinders called fibers. You are born with all the muscle fiber you will ever have. Boys are born with more muscle fiber than girls.

As your bones grow longer, your muscle fibers get longer and thicker. During puberty, your muscles thicken quickly and noticeably because of the testosterone in your bloodstream. Your muscle strength depends on how thick your muscle fiber becomes. You can increase the size and strength of your muscles by exercising. But there is a limit to how thick your muscles can grow.

Steroids

A steroid is an artificial hormone—testosterone. When doctors prescribe this drug, it can help people with certain illnesses. Steroids, while making muscles bigger and stronger, have serious side effects—especially for adolescents. Taken improperly, they can make a person dangerously aggressive and irritable, affect the growth of bones and the testicles, change hair growth and cause acne.

Your Body Image

Body image means what *you* think about *your* body. Our bodies are ALL amazing, and as you know, all very different (what a boring world it would be if this was not the case). But what really matters is whether you can appreciate what you have. Many kids look at their bodies and think they are too fat or too short. But are they? There is no ideal weight or height. What you look like depends on your heredity, your gender, your health, your body type, your diet and your activity level. Most boys your age are fairly healthy but spend a bit too much time sitting on their butts playing games, watching TV... Still, compared to the guys you see on TV, you may have less muscle and may not be as tall. Instead of feeling that we are okay just the way we are, we often compare ourselves to athletes or people in the media. There is no "best." If we are healthy but have learned not to like ourselves, we can unlearn some of that by reminding ourselves every time we look into a mirror "I am me. I am unique."

If you think that you or a friend may have a problem with body image or eating, please consider talking to an adult who knows about this aspect of health or contacting a phone help line. Check out the resources on page 57.

Different Strengths

Guys and girls have different strengths after they've gone through puberty. Everyone knows that guys put on more muscle, so that compared to a girl of the same height, weight and build, he would be able to lift more weight and run faster. But girls have their own strength. It's called *adipose* tissue—also known as fat. What does it do? Well, fat is the storage of energy in the body. And because females need more energy for breast-feeding and caring for a newborn, they store more adipose tissue on their upper arms, breasts, thighs and butt. This storage of energy means that a girl can survive things a guy who is her equivalent couldn't. She could survive extreme drought and hunger, extreme heat and cold. It's just a different kind of strength.

6 Skin and Hair

Pubic hair is hair that grows around your genitals and over the pubic bone. At first your pubic hair may be soft, but it will soon become curlier and thicker. Your pubic hair might even be a different color from the hair on your head. You may notice small white bumps, which are the hairs emerging from their follicles.

About the time you first notice pubic hair, you will see more hair on your arms and legs, and underarm hair. After you've finished growing, you might get hair on your chest, shoulders and back. The amount of body hair you get has to do with heredity and nothing else. Some people are just destined to be hairy and some aren't. The same applies to girls. There is no "right" amount of body or facial hair.

Facial Hair

Most guys can hardly wait to get some signs of facial hair. They think, "Finally, I'm growing up!" Facial hair usually starts when they are between 12 and 15 years old.

The first facial hairs grow on the outer corners of your upper lip. This fuzz is usually soft and light-colored. Your mustache will keep growing until it's darker and thicker. Later, your sideburns will form with the same fuzz. You might have a different-colored hair on your face than on your head. Finally, hair grows on your chin. The smooth area of skin at the sides of the chin and on the cheeks sometimes fills in and sometimes doesn't, depending on your genetics.

Your facial hair will continue to get coarser, darker and thicker as you pass your teen years.

Shaving

Some boys and men prefer to shave their facial hair. Others grow a mustache and/or beard. If you decide not to shave, you can keep the hair clean by washing your face frequently. Nobody wants to kiss yesterday's dinner!

If you decide to remove the hair, you will only have to shave now and then, until your hair gets thicker. An electric razor is fast and safe, but it may irritate your skin and it doesn't shave as close as a razor.

If you try a hand razor, use a clean, sharp blade. A dull blade will hurt and cause irritation. Lather your face with warm water and shaving foam (not soap). You can start by shaving in the direction the hair grows, then switch direction. Start at one ear and stroke down toward the chin. Shave your upper lip and then your chin. Afterward, rinse with cold water.

If you nick yourself shaving, put a bit of tissue or toilet paper on the cut to absorb the blood.

Avoid sharing a razor with another person because there is a risk of spreading viruses such as hepatitis C.

Skin and Sweat

Sweat itself doesn't smell bad; it's the bacteria growing in stale sweat that makes teachers open the windows for some air!

Did you know that the skin is the largest organ of your body? And it does a lot of work. The top layer, the epidermis, is a protective layer of dead skin cells that flake off or need to be washed off. The sebaceous glands make an oily substance called *sebum* that gives skin its soft, stretchy feel. Sweat is your body's temperature regulator. It comes from millions of sweat glands all over your body.

During puberty, your body sweats more, produces more sebum and smells different. Your sweat smell changes because nature intended you to have a "sex smell." Each person has an individual smell that can be pleasing to their partner. But that smell is different from body odor, which develops when the sweat stays around too long.

You will notice more sweat on your feet, on your palms (especially when you are nervous), under your arms and around your *groin*. When you perspire, the sweat clings to your skin and underarm hair. Bacteria are attracted to the warm moist areas; they start to grow and smell. But there's an easy solution! When you wash with soap and water, you remove the extra sweat, sebum and dead skin, and you kill the bacteria. Washing your favorite clothes more often is also important. Some people cover up the odor with deodorant or reduce the amount of sweating with antiperspirant.

Pimples and Acne

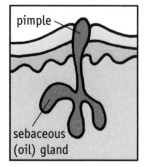

Zits. Everyone would prefer to avoid them, but nearly everyone gets them at some point.

During the teen years a person's skin produces more oil, so you have to live through a "shiny face" and greasier hair stage. What kind of skin you have mainly depends on—you guessed it—heredity. Just like your eye color and height. Let's look at why pimples and *acne* happen and what can be done about it.

When a skin pore becomes clogged with sebum—that oily substance made under the skin—a blackhead forms. When sebum gets trapped beneath the surface of the pore, you get a whitehead. When a whitehead becomes infected, it turns red and fills with pus—a pimple is born. A serious case of blackheads, whiteheads or pimples is called acne.

People born with very curly or kinky hair sometimes get a sore red spot that looks like a zit, but it's just an ingrown hair that needs to be gently tugged out.

There is no guaranteed way to prevent pimples and acne. Squeezing pimples can make the problem worse by causing an infection or scarring. The pimple creams and lotions you see advertised on TV help dry up pimples once you've got them, but they don't prevent acne. Wash your face gently with a pure soap—one without scents and additives—then rinse and dry it well. But don't overdo it.

Doctors used to tell teenagers to stop eating greasy food such as fries, but this is not the cause of pimples. Eating healthy foods, drinking lots of water, getting enough daily exercise and sleep, and avoiding cigarettes all lead to healthier skin, hair, nails and teeth. If your acne is causing you a lot of concern, a skin doctor (called a dermatologist) can give you prescription drugs to help the situation.

Jock Itch

Jock itch is an itchy, red, sore rash on the inner thighs and genitals. It's caused by a fungus that develops when there is no air circulation around your genitals. If you have jock itch, you'll need to get proper medication to make it go away.

You can help avoid the problem by washing your genitals with mild soap and water every day, washing jockstraps frequently and wearing looser underwear.

7 What Happens to Girls?

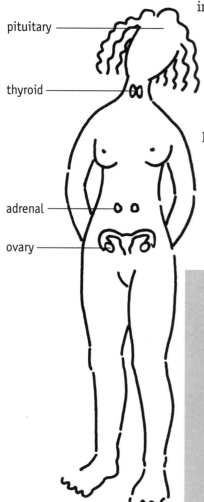

pituitary

thyroid

adrenal

ovary

Why bother to understand what girls go through at puberty? It's important for boys and girls to understand each other because we live in this world together! And while you've known since you were little that girls and boys are different, it's interesting to see how similar we are as well. Also, guys are often somewhat curious about the opposite sex.

Girls start to go through puberty earlier than boys. As you've probably noticed, girls' changes start in two obvious places, their breasts and their height. But just as with boys, each girl goes at her own speed and the process takes years. Puberty starts, as it does for boys, when the pituitary gland sends a message to the sex glands to start making sex hormones. A girl's ovaries start to make the female

What Happens?

Which of these changes of puberty happen only to girls?

- Gets pimples.
- Gets wider shoulders.
- Has a growth spurt.
- Makes sperm.
- Gets a period.
- Gets hair on the face.
- Gets pubic hair, underarm hair and darker leg hair.

- Voice deepens.
- Gets a bigger Adam's apple.
- Grows breasts.
- Develops wider hips.
- Sweats more.
- Gets greasier hair and body odor.
- Has more sexual thoughts.

ANSWER: Only boys make sperm and get bigger Adam's apples and wider shoulders. Only girls get a period, grow breasts and develop wider hips. All the other changes of puberty happen to both boys and girls.

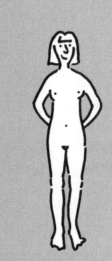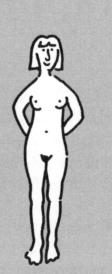

Puberty in Girls

Here are some of the main changes of puberty in girls.

Stage 1.
Her body grows taller. Her hips and thighs get wider.

Stage 2.
Her breasts start to develop, as does pubic hair. Inside a girl's body, her uterus and fallopian tubes get bigger. A small amount of whitish fluid comes from the vagina. As with the male scrotum, her *labia* becomes darker and more distinct.

Stage 3.
Underarm hair, fine upper lip hair and more sweat develop. Arm and leg hair darkens. Her voice becomes a bit deeper. Pimples may start. She is more aware of sexual feelings.

Stage 4.
Her breasts are more developed. She will have started to *menstruate*—get her period.

sex hormones estrogen and progesterone and she will produce a small amount of testosterone. While boys' testosterone levels don't vary that much, girls' hormone levels go through a wild ride every month.

Menstruation

Girls were born with all the ova or eggs ever needed inside their two ovaries. There are hundreds of thousands of them. One egg is called an ovum. Until puberty the eggs are immature. At puberty, hormones make the eggs ripen. About once a month, an egg starts to mature. Usually only one egg matures at a time, but sometimes two or more eggs ripen.

Several days before the egg is released, girls may notice a sort of clear slippery fluid on their underwear or on the toilet paper after they've urinated. This sperm-friendly fluid, or *discharge*, is made by the cervix several days before the egg is released in order to give the sperm a greater chance of surviving while they wait for the egg to show up. Girls can count on getting their period 12 to 14 days after noticing this fluid.

When the egg is ripe, it bursts out of the *ovary*. This is called ovulation. After the egg is released, it travels from the ovary through the fallopian tube to the uterus. At the same time, the lining of the uterus thickens, in case the egg gets fertilized.

If the egg is fertilized by a sperm on its way to the uterus, a new life has started. The embryo will start to grow in the uterus, and it will need the thick, nourishing lining of the uterus. So the woman won't get her period while she is pregnant.

But if the egg has not been fertilized it dissolves within 24 hours and there is no need for the nourishing lining. So, the uterus gets rid of it. This is called a menstrual period, or just a period. The special blood from the uterus flows out of the vagina for two to five days. The cycle is repeated about once a month. Unlike men, women are not able to make babies all their life. Their periods stop when they are in their 50s; and while they can still enjoy sex, they cannot get pregnant after this time called *menopause*.

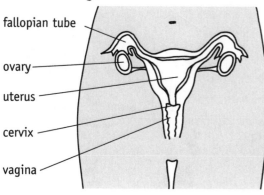

Internal Sex Organs

fallopian tube

ovary

uterus

cervix

vagina

External Genitals

pubic hair

clitoris

urethral opening

vaginal opening

anus

Protection

During her period a girl will use something to catch the flow of special blood. Everyone sees these products on TV ads...but they never say how they work. A pad is made of material that absorbs the flow. It has a sticky strip that adheres to the inside of the girls underpants. She changes her pads regularly, using them until her period stops. A tampon is made of similar material, but it is compressed into a small plug. This fits inside the female's vagina and, again, is changed regularly. Tampons are handy to use during physical activity, especially swimming, but it's up to a girl what she chooses to use.

For some girls having a period is nothing much, but for some it's not that easy. They may experience wild mood swings, sore breasts and bloating before they get their period (called *PMS*). During their period some girls get heavy cramps in their abdomens. It helps if the males around them understand what they are going through.

About Breasts

Guys are generally pretty interested in breasts. So here's the story. On our chest we all have nipples. Nipples, even those of boys, have a network of nerves that make them very sensitive. That's why, when it is cold, or when the nipple is touched, or when a person is thinking about something romantic or exciting, the nipples become harder and erect or pointy. When a girl is between the ages of about 9 and 12 she will notice that one or both of the nipples has become puffy or has a lump under it. (This also happens to around 60 percent of guys for a short time period.) Eventually, the breast tissue will develop further, with a layer of fat on top that makes the breasts the size they are.

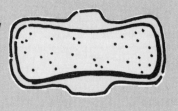

As you know, breasts are for making "milk" for babies. All breasts can do this, no matter what size they are.

Just as guys may wonder about their penis size, girls are often preoccupied with their breast size. If a girl develops faster than her peers she can feel self-conscious and get teased. The same goes if she develops slower. Guys need to think about what it would be like if their penis size was visible for all to comment on!

Do Girls Feel the Same Way as Guys?

While we look quite different, on the inside, guys and girls have much in common. Everyone is kind of excited about not being a little kid anymore. And girls often have the same kinds of questions as guys when they go through puberty. They worry about their breast size and their skin. They wonder if they are attractive; they worry that nobody will like them. They may not understand all their sexual dreams and fantasies. They feel pressure to "fit in." It's important to remember that everyone has lousy days as well as amazing days, no matter what gender they are!

Flirting or Harassment?

Since breasts are so obvious, some guys think that it's okay to make comments about them or other parts of girls' bodies. When comments are made, a female may feel embarrassed and angry, or she may feel flattered. How would a guy know what's okay? Well, it depends on lots of things. Do they know each other? Does she like him? Was the remark meant to be a compliment? If you're not sure, it's best to keep your thoughts to yourself until you are sure!

8 Making Decisions

Having to make decisions is part of life; it also helps you become more mature. And while you may find some decisions easy to make, like doing up your coat when it's cold out—or not—others are tough. It takes practice and learning from our mistakes to get good at making decisions that are best for us.

Ways to Make Decisions

Different people make decisions in different ways. Even for one person, how they decide what to do changes from one situation to the next. So what's the best way to decide something? Well, let's look at a couple of examples.

1. After school your friends ask if you're going to go hang out with them. You really want to, but you had agreed to go home to finish a project you'd been working on. How do you decide what to do? What do you think you would decide? How long would it take to decide?

Here are three different ways that a decision could be made. After reading these, go back and rethink the answers to the questions above.

- **Weigh the consequences:** *"I don't know, I guess it would mostly depend on how much trouble I'd get into if I didn't show up at home."* —K.L., age 16

    What will you miss if you don't go with your friends? How much time have you spent with them lately? How much trouble will you get in at home? Would there be any point trying to call your parents and negotiate with them? What happened the last time you did not follow through with an agreement?

- **Go on impulse**: *"It's easy in this case to like just say 'Sure!' and not really think about it much."* —Jessie, age 13

    You could simply follow your first impulse or thought. This would result in an immediate decision one way or the other.

- **Let someone else decide**: *"I guess I'd call my mom and see if it was okay with her..."* —E.M., age 10

    You could let someone else decide for you. So in this case you may say to your friends, "I don't know, I'm supposed to go right home..." If they say, "okay, see you later..." you go with that; or if they say, "Oh, come on, just for a while..." you go with that; or if you call your parents and they say, "okay" or "No," you go with that.

Consider the following situations, and think of the three (or more) ways that someone could decide what to do.

2. You have been going out with this person for a couple of months. You really like each other. You've kissed and touched on top of clothes. You're curious to do more but you're not sure...

- **Weigh the consequences**: You can try to figure out what could happen if you go further. Would you just do it or hint about it first? What if it went further than you wanted? What if your boyfriend/girlfriend thought you were weird for doing it or for deciding to wait? What if other people found out?

- **Go on impulse:** You don't spend any time thinking about it—you just react to how you are feeling at the time. This could include many feelings, such as scared, horny, cautious, curious...

- **Let someone else decide:** In this situation you could let the other person make all the moves and just go along with it or you could follow what adults in your life may have told you (for instance, to wait until you are older). You could talk with a friend, sibling or trusted adult and go with what they suggest.

   What do you think you would do? How would you decide? How long would it take you to decide?

3. You're hanging out with some guys and one of them calls someone a "faggot." What are your options?

- **Weigh the consequences:** If you say something about the term being ignorant, homophobic or hateful, others may turn on you or think you're gay, or they may back you up. If you do nothing then the others will think that you agree with that view.

- **Go on impulse:** You can act on the first thing you feel or think.

- **Let someone else decide:** You can see how the rest of the group reacts and side with someone else's response, which could include laughing, making similar comments ("Yeah, the queer") or challenging the statement ("What's your problem?", "It's not a disease you know," "Hey, watch your mouth, my cousin's gay"...).

What do you think you would do? How would you decide? How long would it take you to make your decision?

So What's Right?

Making a decision is like dropping a stone into a pond. The ripples it creates in the water spread all the way out, touching everything in their path, long after the stone disappears. How you decide something affects you and the people in your life. So you owe it to yourself to learn how to make the best decisions you can at a given time—and then learn from them.

All of the decisions would be based on your values (what's important to you), past experiences and how much practice you've had at making decisions. How long it takes to make a decision often depends on the kind of thing you have to decide about. In the examples above, numbers 1 and 3 are often made in seconds, but for number 2 the person may need—and should take—more time.

Remember, you can always say, "I have to think about it." *If you're feeling rushed into something, it's hard to do what's right for you.*

Deciding what's right in a certain situation is not always easy. You do your best with it and later, if you see that it wasn't such a great choice, you do what you can to fix it. It takes a lot of courage and wisdom to go back and say, "I don't think that was the best decision. I want to try again."

You're at a Party...

One of the things that happens more as you get older is guy/girl parties. No more loot bags! Parties can be fun, but they can also be awkward. Sometimes someone sneaks alcohol into a party, or they drink it not far from where the party is being held. It's fairly predictable that people around you will be involved with alcohol (same goes for cigarettes) at some point, so if you're the kind of person who chooses to make an informed decision, here's some information you may not already know.

- Alcohol affects people differently depending on their body size, genetics (some of us don't process alcohol very easily), if their stomach is full or empty, their emotional state, other drug use and if they drink regularly.
- Drinking (beer, wine or hard liquor) helps most people feel less anxious. This is one of the reasons some people (of all ages) drink when they party. After a while, however, drinking can also make people feel sleepy, aggressive or depressed.
- Alcohol is highly addictive. The addiction tends to run in families.
- You can drink and not feel much of an effect and then—*wham!*—your world is spinning, you can't speak or walk properly and you may feel like you're going to barf.
- Nobody can give consent for any sexual activity if they are drunk.
- Two dangerous things about heavy drinking at a party are alcohol poisoning, which requires hospitalization, and drowning in your vomit if you pass out on your back.

If you decide to drink alcohol, reduce your risks by having a meal first, don't accept drinks from someone unknown to you, take it slow, if you feel sick *don't* go off on your own and lie down and *do* call in an adult for help if things get out of control.

No Questions Asked

Some families have a "no questions asked" rule. If a kid finds himself in an uncomfortable or dangerous situation, he can call a parent or designated adult for a drive home, any time of the night, no questions asked—for 24 hours.

9 More about Sex

Attractions

"How do you know when someone likes you?" —GRADE 6 CLASS
"When you like a girl, how do you get them to like you back?" —BOYS'
GROUP, AGES 11–13

Sexual attractions are a big part of growing up. When you're first
going through puberty you may be hot for a musician, an actor, an
older sibling's friend or even a teacher! Adults sometimes call this a
"crush." Often you never let the other person know about it, but it's
fun to fantasize or daydream about being with them.

At some point it's likely that you will become attracted to someone whom you actually could be involved with. When you're around that
person, you'll feel a bit sweaty and warm, you may become aware of new
feelings in your genitals, you'll want to look good when the person is
around and you may be shyer or more rowdy than usual. If the other person likes you, the same things happen to them. There may be lots of
online flirting and your ear will get hot from all the phone chats! It feels
good and exciting to have someone like you. You just have to make sure
you don't stop spending time with other friends or doing your work at
home and school.

Relationships

Being in love and having a good relationship are not always the same
thing. Think about the relationships you have with friends, family members or a boyfriend/girlfriend. Below name four characteristics or things
that are part of a healthy relationship.

- _____
- _____
- _____
- _____

Going Out

"When I was in Grade 7, I was going out with this girl...it felt so weird!" —M.M., AGE 18

At some point when two people like each other they feel a pressure to say they are "going out," or a similar term. If you're in high school (and your parents don't forbid it), then one-to-one time can be comfortable. But before that time, as M.M. discovered, it's often just plain weird. What can be more comfortable at this age is just hanging out in a group together. This way you can joke, flirt and get used to the whole romance thing without wondering what you should do together or how far to go sexually.

More than 50 percent of young people wait to have sex until after they are 17 years old.

You're on the right track if you put a bunch of the following points: honesty, trust, making each other laugh, shared values, some similar interests, respect, not afraid to disagree, can solve problems together and, if sexual interest is part of the deal, enjoyment of physical sharing—without high risks.

a good question

"How do you know when you're in love?"
—GRADE 7 CLASS

Being in love is a feeling. You get excited or horny, you think about the person all the time, you feel a bit crazy... It can happen in an instant. Falling out of love can also happen in an instant. This can happen to people of all ages. Real *love* is a verb—an action word. It involves all parts of you. It takes time and doesn't just come or go.

More Than Kiss

There are laws about how old you have to be to have sexual intercourse. What is it for your area?

Messing around, making out, touching—these are things teens may do when they are turned on but not ready for sexual intercourse. A very common and important question is, "When is the right time for sex?"

What do you think? Do you know what your parents would say? Do you know what the law says?

Unlike what you see on TV, some young people do remain virgins until they're married. Some want to wait until finishing high school. Many people say they'd wait until they "felt ready," which partly means being in a trusting relationship. Your parents will likely hope you are at least 30 years old! While no single opinion is right for everyone, youth who have intercourse before they have turned 16 are much more likely to regret it, especially girls. Waiting until you are older is not always easy these days, but teens who have good information and goals for their future often make that choice. The next section looks at some of the not-so-great things that can happen involving sex.

Sexual Abuse

Sometimes girls and boys are forced, tricked or bribed into sexual touching or sexual activities, including being used for *pornography* (porn). The abuser is usually someone older or more powerful whom the child knows. It may be a family member, friend of the family, neighbor, babysitter—anybody really. Any type of intimate sexual contact with children is called sexual abuse and it's illegal. Kids often wait until they are older before telling someone about the abuse.

There are many reasons for this:

- They may have felt that it was their fault. It is **NEVER** the child's fault, but the abuser may convince them that it is.
- They may have been threatened or bribed into keeping the secret.
- Because it had to do with sex they may have just been very confused and embarrassed.
- They may have tried to tell someone but were not believed.

We all need to have positive, loving physical interaction every day. Since sexual abuse doesn't always hurt physically, it can be confusing. If you have had anything sexual happen to you that made you feel uncomfortable, please speak to an adult about it. Teachers, camp counselors and

child care and youth leaders are trained about abuse. They will reassure
you that it was not your fault. Also, it's only when someone tells their
secret that the abusers will be stopped. There are confidential phone
lines (see page 57) you can call, where you don't even have to give your
name or phone number.

Sexual Assault

While it is mainly men
who sexually assault
others, most men are
not abusers.

While we often hear in the news about teens being sexually
assaulted when they were walking down the street at
nights or going into a building, the fact is most assaults
happen from people we know. Any unwanted sexual kissing or touching, whether there is forced intercourse or
not, is a form of sexual assault. That means there is
no *consent*. Forced intercourse is often called *rape*.

The truth is that for teens and adults, sexual
assault usually involves someone we are going out
with or living with or even married to.

Say you were with someone alone because you
thought you might make out a bit. If the guy decided
he wanted to go further, regardless of how the girl
felt, he probably wouldn't use physical force right
away—he'd start with his words. He might say, "You're
so sexy, what are you going to do now that you've
turned me on?" Or, "I thought you really liked me."
Or girls may say to guys, "What's the matter, are
you gay?"

When someone is drunk they cannot give consent, no matter what their sex or age.

Sometimes girls feel guilty when they end up doing something sexual they didn't want to do. They think, "Maybe it's because of the way I was dressed. Maybe it's because I went somewhere private. Maybe it's because I was drinking." The point is that even if a girl *might* have protected herself better, *she didn't commit the crime*—the guy did.

If you have been involved with any form of sexual assault—please talk to someone about it (see page 57).

STIs

As you know from the other chapters, when a male and female (before menopause) have sexual intercourse it can result in a pregnancy. The other thing all people, of all ages, who are having sex need to know about are sexually transmitted infections, or *STIs*. They are also referred to as diseases (STDs). Let's look briefly at what these are, how you get them, how you know if you have one, what they can do to you and how to avoid them.

There are two basic kinds of STIs. The ones caused by bacteria can be cured with medication. Those caused by a virus can't be cured with medication but can be treated to reduce their effect on a person. Here are a few of the most common STIs:

Bacteria	Virus
Chlamydia	HPV (human papilloma virus)
Gonorrhea	Herpes
Syphilis	Hepatitis B
	HIV (human immunodeficiency virus)

How You Get Them

As the name says, these infections are passed or transmitted from one infected person to their partner during certain kinds of sexual contact. You don't get these through hugging, kissing or touching with your hands. Unprotected vaginal and anal intercourse (the anus is the bum hole) are the easiest forms of transmission.

While HIV (the virus that causes AIDS—acquired immune deficiency syndrome) is transmitted through unprotected sexual intercourse, there are other ways of getting it. It can easily be passed between people who share needles, including tattoo needles and the ink. It can also be passed from an infected mother to her baby—although if the mother gets on special AIDS medication the chance of this happening is small.

How a Person Knows They Are Infected

One of the problems when a person gets an STI is that they often don't know they have it. Some people do get symptoms (a symptom shows you have something—for example, a symptom of a cold is a runny nose). Those lucky enough to have a symptom may notice a discharge from the vagina or urethra, or sores or bumps on their genitals. Yuck!

However, many people never have obvious signs of illness. When a person gets HIV, they can feel fine for *years* before noticing symptoms. So how can you know? The only way someone can know for sure that they have an STI is to get tested at a medical clinic.

What Can STIs Do to You?

If you have an STI or genital irritation and have unprotected sex you are at much higher risk for getting HIV.

If a person has one of the bacterial infections, he or she can take antibiotics and be cured. If they are *not* treated, the infection could lead to more serious problems.

With viruses there is good and bad news. Most young people these days are vaccinated against *hepatitis B* so they probably won't get it. HPV can just cause bothersome wart-like bumps on the skin, but depending on the type, it can cause cancer of the cervix, especially for girls who have unprotected sex from an early age. Fortunately, our immune system can sometimes get rid of HPV on its own. Herpes, which is in the same family as cold sores people get on their lips, can cause painful blisters on and around the genitals. For a pregnant woman, herpes can be extremely dangerous if it's passed on to her baby during the birth.

What about Oral Sex?

Oral sex, which goes by many slang terms including "going down" and "*blow jobs*," means putting the mouth on another person's genitals. It is not possible to get pregnant through this form of sex, but it is possible to transmit STIs.

What about AIDS?

When a person has HIV and then develops AIDS, their immune system is no longer working properly. This means that diseases their body would normally fight could end up killing them. Fortunately in many (but not all) countries, people can get medication that helps them live much longer. However, because of all the side effects from the medication itself, AIDS is very hard to live with at times and there is no cure. Remember, you will not get HIV if you go to school with, live with or care for someone who has the disease.

Protection

The best way to avoid getting an STI is to avoid risky sexual activities. Not having sexual intercourse, often called abstinence, obviously reduces the chance of getting an infection. Hugging, kissing and touching with hands are all safe as well.

When people have sexual intercourse they can reduce the risk of getting an STI by using protection. You've got it—condoms. When used properly every time, condoms are very effective at stopping the spread of STIs, including HIV. There are other ways to make sex safer and it's the responsibility of anyone having sex to become well informed.

Birth Control

Most of the time when a man and woman have sex, it is because it feels good, not because they want to make a baby. So unless they want a baby, every time a couple has intercourse they must use some form of *birth control*.

Condoms and birth control pills are two methods of protection commonly used by young people. The male condom, which is like a narrow balloon, is rolled down over the erect penis. It catches the semen (and any infected fluid) before it enters the vagina. Birth control pills work mainly by stopping the egg from being released. They don't protect against STIs. There are other forms of birth control that use hormones as well.

No method works 100 percent of the time except not having sexual intercourse.

The Morning-After Pill

Females who have had unprotected sexual intercourse can use an ECP—emergency contraceptive pill. It is also called the morning-after pill. It should be taken as soon as possible after unprotected sex but can be used up to five days after. Again, it doesn't work all the time.

When a pregnancy does happen by accident, the girl or woman has three choices. She can carry on with the pregnancy and then either keep the baby or give it up for adoption. Or she can end the pregnancy with an *abortion*. None of these three options are easy so it's highly recommended that, especially for young people, they talk to a trusted adult. As long as they don't worry about being punished, girls will often go to someone in their family. They can also go to a teen clinic, go to a teacher or call a hotline. See page 57 for more details.

Where to Go for More Help

We've given you some information about the sexual part of life, but you probably have many more questions. On page 57, you'll find some suggestions about where else to go for more info. The computer you're working on may block a search that includes any sex-related words, so ask an adult for help if possible. If you're unsure about any answer, keep checking until you feel more certain!

For More Information

Books

Harris, Robie H. *It's So Amazing: A Book about Eggs, Sperm, Birth, Babies and Families.* Candlewick Press, 2002.

Wolf, Anthony. *Get Out of My Life—But First Could You Drive Me and Cheryl to the Mall?* New York: The Noonday Press, 1991.

Web Sites

www.kidshealth.org
In English and Spanish, for pre-teens, teens and parents. Many topics are covered.

www.sexualityandyou.ca
In English and French, for teens, parents and health educators.

www.teenwire.com
In English and Spanish, primarily for teens.
Provided by Planned Parenthood of America.

Videos/Films

Changes series. National Film Board of Canada. Inexpensive, Grades 4–6.

Talking about Sex: A Guide for Parents. Planned Parenthood of America (1-800-669-0156).

Phone Hotlines

Kids Help Phone
1-800-668-6868 (in Canada)
Free and confidential—any topic.

Childhelp U.S.A.
1-800-422-4453 (in the United States)
Child abuse hotline.

Parents' Help Line
1-888-603-9100 (in Canada)
Professionals available for any topic.
You can also call your local public health or Planned Parenthood office for help.

Glossary

abortion *(uh-BORE-shun)*: a medical procedure to end a pregnancy.

acne *(AK-nee)*: a bad case of pimples.

adipose *(ADD-uh-pose)*: fatty tissue.

adolescence *(add-o-LESS-sens)*: the stage of life between childhood and adulthood.

adolescent *(add-o-LESS-sent)*: a person going through adolescence.

amniotic fluid *(am-nee-AH-tik FLOO-id)*: the liquid that surrounds the unborn baby in the uterus.

ampulla *(am-POOL-uh)*: the place where mature sperm are stored until they are ejaculated.

anal intercourse *(AY-nul IN-ter-kors)*: when the penis is inserted into the anus of a partner.

anorexia *(ah-nor-REX-ee-ah)*: a serious illness in which girls or boys starve themselves.

anus *(AY-nus)*: the opening where feces (poop) leave the body.

areola *(ah-REE-oh-luh)*: the ring of skin around the nipple.

aroused *(ah-RAU-zd)*: feeling sexual excitement.

asshole *(AZ-hole)*: slang for anus.

balls *(BALZ)*: slang for testes.

birth control *(BURTH CON-troll)*: methods used to prevent pregnancy.

bisexual *(bye-SEX-shu-hul)*: an orientation or attraction toward both males and females.

bladder *(BLADD-her)*: a sac inside the body that holds urine.

blow job *(BLO jobb)*: slang for oral sex.

boner *(BOH-nur)*: slang for erection.

boobs or boobies *(BOOBZ or BOO-bees)*: slang for breasts.

bowel movement *(BOW-ell MOOF-ment)*: solid waste that leaves through the anus.

breast *(BREST)*: the milk-producing glands of a woman, or the chest of a man.

cervix *(SIR-vicks)*: the lower part of the uterus.

cesarean *(si-ZAR-ee-en)*: surgical operation to remove a baby from the uterus.

circumcised *(sir-kum-SIZED)*: a penis with the foreskin removed.

circumcision *(sir-kum-SISH-un)*: the operation to remove the foreskin of the penis.

clitoris *(KLIT-or-is)*: a sensitive organ, seen on the outside above a girl's urinary opening.

coke *(KOKE)*: slang for the drug cocaine.

come or cum *(CUHM)*: slang for semen.

conception *(kon-SEP-shun)*: the joining of the female egg and the male sperm to make a new life.

condom *(KON-dum)*: a tube made of latex rubber or other material that is rolled onto the penis before sexual intercourse to prevent disease and pregnancy.

consent *(KON-cent)*: to agree to something.

crack *(KRAK)*: slang for a powerful form of the drug cocaine.

dick *(DIK)*: slang for penis.

discharge *(DISS-charj)*: fluid or mucus from a body opening or sore.

dope *(DOHP)*: slang for marijuana.

ejaculate *(ee-JACK-you-lat)*: semen.

ejaculation *(ee-JACK-you-lay-shun)*: when semen comes out of the penis.

embryo *(EM-bree-oh)*: the name for an unborn baby for the nine weeks after conception.

epididymis *(e-pee-DID-i-muss)*: a group of tiny tubes attached to the testicles where sperm mature.

erection *(ee-REK-shun)*: when the penis fills with blood and becomes stiff and hard.

erotic *(ee-ROT-ick)*: books, movies or feelings about sexual matters.

estrogen *(ES-tro-jen)*: the female sex hormone made mainly in the ovaries.

fallopian tubes *(fuh-LOPE-ee-un)*: the narrow tubes between the ovaries and the uterus.

female *(FEE-mail)*: women or girls.

fertilization *(fur-till-eye-ZAY-shun)*: when the egg and sperm join to start a new life.

fetus *(FEET-us)*: the name for an unborn baby from nine weeks after conception until its birth.

flaccid *(FLA-sid)*: soft or limp.

fooling around *(FU-ling uh-ROWND)*: slang for sexual touching or sexual intercourse.

foreskin *(FOUR-skin)*: the skin around the head of the penis.

French kissing *(FRENCH KISS-sing)*: when partners put their tongues into each other's mouth.

gay *(GHAY)*: common word for male homosexual.

gender *(JEN-duhr)*: being male or female.

genes *(JEANS)*: the part of each cell that carries inherited traits on to the next generation.

genitals *(JEN-a-tulls)*: the outside sex organs of both males and females.

glands *(GLAN-dz)*: a part of the body that makes secretions such as hormones and milk.

glans *(GLANZ)*: the head of the penis.

groin *(GROI-n)*: the area around the genitals.

hepatitis B *(HEP-uh-TIE-tiss bee)*: a virus that affects the liver; it can be spread by unprotected sex or shared needles.

heredity *(hair-ED-i-tee)*: the characteristics of your family that are passed to you at conception.

heterosexual *(HET-er-oh-SEK-shoo-ul)*: someone who is emotionally and sexually attracted to people of the opposite sex.

homosexual *(HOME-oh-SEK-shoo-ul)*: someone who is emotionally and sexually attracted to people of the same sex.

hormones *(HOAR-moans)*: chemical messengers that tell parts of your body to do something.

horny *(HOAR-nee)*: slang for arousal or wanting sex.

hymen *(HI-mun)*: a ring of skin that may partly cover the vaginal opening.

jerking off or jacking off *(JURHK-king or JAKK-king)*: slang for masturbation.

labia *(LAY-bee-ah)*: the folds of skin around the opening of the vagina.

larynx *(LARR-inks)*: the part of the throat containing the vocal cords.

lesbian *(LEZ-bee-an)*: common word for female homosexual.

lips—i.e., inner lips and outer lips *(LIPZ)*: other words for labia.

making out *(MAY-king out)*: slang for sexual touching.

male *(MAIL)*: men or boys.

mammary glands *(MA-muh-ree GLAN-dz)*: the milk-making glands in the breast.

masturbation *(mass-tur-BAY-shun)*: rubbing the genitals for sexual pleasure.

menopause *(MEHN-oh-paws)*: a woman's final menstrual period.

menstruation *(men-strew-AY-shun)*: the monthly shedding of the lining of the uterus.

miscarriage *(MISS-care-ridge)*: a spontaneous abortion of a fetus.

nipple *(NIP-pull)*: the small raised part in the center of the breast.

oral sex *(OR-ull seks)*: when one partner puts his or her mouth on the genitals of the other.

orgasm *(OR-gaz-um)*: an intense whole-body feeling at the height of sexual excitement.

orientation *(OR-ree-en-TAY-shun)*: whom a person is emotionally and sexually attracted to.

ova *(OH-vah)*: the female egg cells.

ovary *(OH-vah-ree)*: the gland that makes female sex hormones and egg cells.

ovulation *(OV-you-lay-shun)*: the release of a mature egg from the ovary.

penis *(PEE-niss)*: the tube-like sex organ of males, which hangs outside their bodies.

period *(PEER-ee-id)*: menstruation.

pituitary gland *(pi-TYOU-uh-terr-ee)*: a gland in the brain that makes hormones.

placenta *(plah-SEN-tah)*: an organ that connects the mother to the unborn baby.

PMS or premenstrual syndrome *(PREE-mehn-strul)*: a group of physical and/or emotional changes some women experience 3 to 14 days before their period.

pornography *(por-NOG-ra-fee)*: pictures and/or film that have a sexual content that is intended to cause sexual arousal; also called "adult entertainment."

pregnant *(PREGG-nunt)*: having an embryo or fetus growing in the uterus.

progesterone *(PRO-jes-ter-own)*: a female sex hormone.

prostaglandins *(PROST-uh-glan-dins)*: a hormone that makes the uterus muscle tighten.

prostate gland *(PROSS-tate)*: a male gland near the bladder that adds fluid to semen.

puberty *(PEW-burr-tee)*: the physical and emotional changes during adolescence.

pubic hair *(PEW-bik)*: the hair that grows around the genitals.

rape *(RAYP)*: forced sexual intercourse.

rectum *(REK-tum)*: the last section of the intestines where bowel movements pass through the body.

reproduction *(ree-pro-DUCK-shun)*: creating life.

reproductive organs *(ree-pro-DUCK-tiv OR-guns)*: sex organs needed to make babies.

scrotum *(SKROW-tum)*: the soft sac in males that holds the testes.

sebum *(SEE-bum)*: the oily substance made in the sebaceous glands.

secretion *(suh-CREE-shun)*: a fluid that comes from the body.

semen *(SEE-mun)*: the whitish liquid that males ejaculate, made from sperm and fluid.

seminal vesicles *(SEM-i-nul VES-i-kuls)*: two structures that produce a fluid that helps make up semen in a male.

sex *(SEKS)*: male or female; also a common term for sexual intercourse.

sex organs *(SEKS OR-guns)*: the penis and testicles in the male; the ovaries, uterus, vulva and breasts in females.

sexual assault *(a-SAWLT)*: unwanted sexual touching, including rape.

sexual harassment *(huh-RASS-ment)*: being bothered by someone in a sexual way.

sexual intercourse *(IN-ter-kors)*: when the penis enters the vagina.

sexuality *(sek-shoo-AL-li-tee)*: feelings and attitudes about your sexual self—lasts all your life.

smegma *(SMEG-muh)*: a secretion from the glans that allows the foreskin to move easily.

sperm *(SPURM)*: the male sex cell needed to make a baby.

sterile *(STAIR-ul)*: not able to produce a child.

stillbirth *(STIHL-burth)*: when a baby is born after dying inside the uterus.

STIs or sexually transmitted infections *(in-FEX-shuns)*: germs that can be passed on during sexual activity.

straight *(STRATE)*: slang term for heterosexual person.

sweat glands *(SWETT)*: the parts of your body that regulate body temperature.

testes *(TES-teez)*: the testicles.

testicles *(TES-ti-kuls)*: male sex glands that make sex hormones and sperm.

testis *(TES-tis)*: one testicle.

testosterone *(tes-TOS-tur-own)*: a male sex hormone.

transsexual or transgender *(tranz-SEKS-shul or tranz-JEN-duhr)*: also called "trans," people who cross the boundaries of the sex and/or gender they were given at time of birth.

umbilical cord *(um-BILL-i-cul)*: the cord connecting an unborn baby to the placenta.

urethra *(you-REE-thrah)*: the tube through which urine (and semen, in males) leaves the body.

urine *(YUR-in)*: body waste from the bladder—pee.

uterus *(YOU-ter-us)*: the hollow muscular organ that holds and nourishes an unborn baby.

vagina *(VAH-jeye-nah)*: the stretchy passageway of muscles that joins the uterus to outside the body.

vas deferens *(VAZ DEF-eh-renz)*: the small tube where sperm travel from the testicles.

vulva *(VUL-vah)*: the outside sex organs of a female.

wet dream *(WHET dreem)*: an ejaculation that happens while a boy sleeps.

yeast infection *(YEEST in-FEX-shun)*: an overgrowth of healthy organisms in the vagina, which causes unusual discharge and/or discomfort; it can be passed on during sex but is not an STI.

Index